The Scent of the Clouds

Poems, Prose, and Persian Proverbs

Melody Khosravi

Copyright © 2019 Melody Khosravi

All rights reserved.

ISBN: 978-1-0903-4856-2

Dedicated to you

Do you think that each cloud in the sky
Might smell like a loved one as they passed by
On their way to heaven; to paradise?

- the scent of the clouds

Chō istadeyi, daste oftade gir

"As long as you are standing, give a hand to those who have fallen"

There comes a time
In everyone's mind
When you feel a little blue
But it seems to me
That lately
This turned out to be always true
At first the blue was like the sky
With white clouds coming in
And stopping by
But then the storms
The lightening
Its roars
Made it quite dark blue
Then one day
The clouds went away
And other colors came rushing too
I looked for what
Could have colored my thoughts
And that's when I saw you

- 	thank you

I looked out the window
My plane flew so fast
I was so excited
To see new lands
I wanted a token
From everywhere I went
I couldn't wait to get there
I even had a plan
I'd stop by Egypt first
To see a mummy or two
I'd love to see Giza
The tomb of Khufu
Then comes Syria
And of course Iraq
There's so many places
I couldn't just stop
At one place
There's so much to see
I looked out my window
Maybe I'll be
Able to see some of Palestine too
I heard there's some tension
I hope it'll conclude
I look out my window
Nothing's there anymore
There is no more Giza
There are no more stores
There's nothing left but sand and some blood
Was I too late?
I leave the plane
I start to run
I cry
In disbelief at what has become
Of the beautiful Middle East
It is all undone
If this is Egypt I am scared to see
What has become of Yemen

Or of Turkey
Is Iran still there?
Can I still see Kuwait?
Oh why did I not come sooner?
Why did I wait?
The year is almost 3001
I look around for someone
Anyone
Who could tell me that this is all a lie
A joke
A prank
From a semi-wise guy
My heart sinks further as I turn around
A small little boy comes to me
And frowns
They came like you, he said
In those big flying boxes
They took our homes
Our families
Our trust and
They told us they were trying to help
But they lied
My mother has cried so much she is blind
Why did you do this to us?
What had we done?
I miss my father
My brothers
Now I'm the only son
I hug him tight and I cry
And I cry
Oh why did I
Not come sooner
I should have tried

    -    the year 3001

It isn't how I love him
It isn't why I smile
It isn't my heart aching
When I don't see him for a while
It isn't that I'm lonely
Or that he makes me glow
I know I shouldn't love him
But why I do,
I'll never know

- common sense, where are you?

When God created you He said,
"This one will be perfect
Her love will have no end"
He let you down gently
From the heavens above
And slowly you breathed
While a hundred white doves
Crowded around you
As you made your entrance
Unto this Earth
Of blood
Lies
And vengeance
The angels kept looking down without ease
To make sure you were safe
And God was so pleased
Even though around you
Was war and betrayal
You loved and cared to no avail
When a hundred white doves
Returned back to Earth
To bring you home
You sighed and said first
That you wanted to leave
A small gift for someone
And that's when you left your love
In your daughter and your son

      -      mothers

Choōbe Khoda seda nadare

"God's cane is silent"

In your happiness, I might forget your cheers
In your sadness, I might forget your sorrows
In your anger, I will remember your words
In your anger, your words have thorns
I listen
I bleed

- the hidden truth

There are times in your life that you will lose your sanity
You might have misplaced it or forgot to hold on to it
It might have been stripped from you or someone might have claimed it
If this happens do not be afraid
Do not panic
The thing with sanity is that it always comes back
In the form of friendships
In the form of your mother's laugh
In the form of your father's jokes
In the form of a new romance
In the form of a new book
It comes back
It comes back

- crazy

I heard you were looking for me
In the meadows of your memories
In the fields of your thoughts
In the pools of your dreams
Do you not know where I am?
Or have you forgotten
That I am the song you sing in the shower
The food you like to order all the time
The show you watch to comfort you at night
I am all of the favorites in your life
I am the feeling of satiety
I have never gone anywhere, darling
As long as there is pain
I am the pleasure of taking it away

-     your favorite thing

False beliefs and greed will blind men
Into thinking
The blood of my womb
Is the ink of their pen

- dear senator

To mourn someone who is not dead
Is a painful curse it must be said
Death is a fate that is equal to all
But parting in life is not simple or small
You wonder where or who they are with
You yearn for their touch or their lips on your breath
So to mourn someone who is not dead
Is a grief that I truly do dread

-     rip

If this is what it has come to
Where I must dream to see your smile
Where I must dream to feel your touch
Where I must dream to hear your laugh
And only in my dreams will you stay
And only then will we grow old together
Then I wish a thousand years of sleep
And a thousand more
And a thousand more

    -    please don't wake me up

Har chē pish ayad, khosh ayad

"*All that comes is welcome*"

I know there is always a better tomorrow ahead
When I think of the grief of yesterday
And it makes me grateful for today

- thankful

Do not think that your shouts were unheard by he who was silent. Guilt has ears but shame has no tongue. So do not yell louder. Heal harder. Then live in peace.

- the recipe

If only you forgave yourself like you forgave him
Imagine what could happen
Forgiveness given to someone deserving

- imagine

What good does your apology
When it is not my foot you have stepped on
But my trust and dignity?

- not enough

Yē dast seda nadare

"A single hand makes no noise"

Each wave that washes upon the shore
Comes back
For it is meant to be this way
Therefore the shore does not chase each wave
For it knows it is meant to come back
And that which is meant to be
Does not need chasing

-     kismet

No winter lasts forever
Spring will always come

- norooz

I stopped wishing for him to have a daughter one day
When I realized he was my father's karma
For all that happened to my mama

- I pray he never has a daughter

With our greeting translated to "peace be upon you"
You will know all that there is to know of our people

- salam

Hich arzāni bi elat nist

"Nothing is cheap for no reason"

Become a good memory
Even if they betray you
Humiliate you
Become a good memory
So that when they speak of goodness
Of love
Of kindness
Their eyes scream out your name
Become a good memory

- they won't ever be able to hide you

Her beauty has aged
But her hope remains
And that is why she is beautiful
Sometimes she cries
And she hurts inside
But she is still very beautiful
She's been robbed
And stabbed
Kind of hard
Kind of bad
But she is still beautiful
Her future is on trial
She hasn't laughed
Or danced
In awhile
But she is still beautiful
Why? She asks
Do you not see my wrinkles?
My tears of pain?
I have grown old
And will not be youthful again
I caressed her cheek
She smiled at me
In all her grief
She smiled at me
And that is why she is beautiful

- iran

Bā yek gol, bahar nemishavad

- *"A single flower does not make spring"*

Friendship is the most romantic relationship there is. It is the bond of two souls who owe each other nothing. Absolutely nothing. Neither physical obligations nor financial ones. They are simply souls that enjoy each other. Nothing more nothing less. Its impression lasts a lifetime and its contract is empowerment. There are no vows to be said. No legal documents to create. Not even a surname to change. It is just you. It is just them.

- the most powerful

Too many times
You have announced me as your religion
Without even knowing how to pray

- blasphemy

He who was silent
While you screamed
Spoke louder than you

- deafening

In your most difficult hour, when you feel like giving up
Remember your children and grandchildren are watching
That very hour will one day be the memory you tell them
Make it a story of triumph

-     they are listening

Never place your comfort in two things:
Materialistic objects and people
They both come and go
But the worst of the two
Are people
For neither a house nor a car will get up one day and leave

- beware

How we treat others in love
Speaks loudly of how much we love ourselves
Tell me, why do you hate yourself so?

- I love myself

Bēkhand ta donya be rooyat bēkhande

"Laugh so that the world laughs with you"

There will come a time in your life when your morals and values will be questioned. You will be faced with the dilemma of doing one of two things: what you feel in your bones to be right or what is easiest to do. Ultimately, it will be your choice. But remember, our bones will ache with old age. And each ache will be a chime; a reminder of that day.

-     brittle

The soil of your land is not better than mine
Nor is my fruit sweeter than yours
Do not buy the lies they try to sell
All the land upon this Earth
Has but only one Farmer

- harvest love

My condolences to the children of
Palestine
Iraq
Syria
Afghanistan
Yemen
Libya
And any other child on this Earth
Who was robbed of their childhood
A felony no one deserves to fall victim to
A crime I would not wish on my worst enemy

-    remember them

If women have been punished since the dawn of time
Simply for biting into forbidden fruit
Then I wonder what the punishment for men will be
Once God has seen all they have done

-       apple

Tā tavāni deli be dast āvar ke del shekastan honar nemibāshad

"Win over as many hearts as you can, for breaking one is no art"

To lie is easy
But to speak the truth
Is a battle even the strongest of men
Have lost

       -       cowards

Some people will say, "I love you"
And by them saying it
They will have tarnished the beauty of those words
For those words have power and dignity
It was never meant for just any tongue to say
Or ear to hear

- choose carefully

The past is not a good place to live in
But it can be a wonderful place to vacation in
Stroll through sweet memories and taste the warmth of their love on your tongue
Camp under the lessons it taught you and listen to the howling of the tears you had shed
Swim in the crystal clear lakes of the laughter you shared
And breathe in the luscious air of your growth
Your stay should be brief
And remember that the past should not haunt you
Or scare you
Or bring you sadness
It should be a place to visit once in awhile
To prepare for your future
And to remind you in your present moment
Where you have come from

- safe travels

What I allow
Is what comes to me
If I allow disrespect
It is at my front door
If I allow anger
It will park in my driveway
I'd much rather have peace
And love
And hope as neighbors

- my neighborhood

A guilt-free conscience
And some peace of mind
Are luxuries that he can't find
Within the walls of the lies he's built

- treasures

Kooh be kooh nemiresad, ādam be ādam miresad

"*Mountains do not meet, but people do*"

Forgiving yourself is the hardest thing to do sometimes
For it is not always anger or pride that gets in our way
But shame
For we listened to the softer voice within us
When the louder voice pleaded us to not do it
To not listen
To not trust
To not give a second chance
We heard that voice loud and clear
And still ignored it

-     forgive me

I cannot think of something more disastrous
Than misplacing your happiness in someone else's hands
Hands that might be dirty
Hands that might drop it
Hands that could crush it

- take it back

My father's smile and my mother's ease
Are things
That I will fight everyday to keep
To protect
To see

- they deserve the world

It is not your fault
That you love too hard
Nor is it wrong
I was once like you
Once in a blue moon
I truly thought that we had belonged
But never fret
It's not over yet
You'll find love one day
You're not meant to be
With someone who barely
Responds to your love
The same way

- you deserve more

I wish the human language did not include words for "apology"
or "sorry"
And allowed us humans to show it rather than say it
How different this world would be

-     talk is cheap

Doōroogh goo kam hāfeze ast

"A liar has terrible memory"

Hagh bē haghdar miresad

"*Justice will serve he who is deserving*"

I have felt safest
In the arms of the ones who hurt me the most
Now tell me,
Whose arms can I trust now?

-     bitter irony

Mirrors are peculiar things
You expect to see what is there
But you would not believe how many times
I did not recognize
The face that stared back at me

- reflection

Our tears have a higher purpose in life:
To shed at the sight of breathtaking art
And impeccable films
To welcome the birth of new life
Or to mourn the loss of one
And to think that I,
Wasted all of mine on you
What a loss of pureness
What a loss

- a shame

Do not pick up what has fallen on the floor unless you are absolutely sure it is clean. Who knows what it could do to you.

- second chances

Some folks are afraid of loving too hard
They're scared of heartbreak
Of going too far
Now I won't lie, it does hurt a lot
When the one you love
Shreds your heart apart
But now that it has happened to me
I have some wise words
Come sit
And you'll see
That when I say
To lose in love
Is not a loss
You grow stronger
And braver
You become the boss
Of your happiness
Laughter
You love yourself first
You make time for you
It won't matter what hurts
Because after the heartaches
Of them saying goodbye
You realize that you truly did try
But now it is time to seek love again
It is time to flourish
And be your own friend
I hope you get what I'm trying to say
If it's meant to be
Know that they will stay
And if they don't
And they walk away
Well good riddance
Who needs them anyway?

- the most important relationship

I have not yet met the woman whom I am destined to be
I know the day I meet her
Will be the best day of my life
To finally hold her in my arms and yell with pure joy
"Where have you been all this time?"
And she will hold me tight and wipe my tears and say
"I was waiting for you, I am so glad you're here"
And she will show me the world through her eyes
A world I once thought I knew
But now has much more color

- the meeting

I was once a bird
Who liked to fly towards the moon
Everyone called me crazy for wanting to touch the moon
In the dark? They said
Why would anyone fly at night when you can fly during the day?
And against my better judgment I listened to them
I listened and flew during the day
And as I tried touching the sun
It burned me
I was once a bird

- choose your own path

I don't ever want to see you beg for love
Be it a mother's
A father's
A lover's
Your love for yourself must be so deep
That you become your own mother
Your own father
Your own lover

- in good company

I have enjoyed the ocean long before I had enjoyed you
And I will enjoy it long after the enjoyment of you
Has been silenced in my veins

- again

Heartbreak sounds beautiful in poems. And in films. And in song. I am here to break this false notion that for some reason was sold to us. Heartbreak is neither beautiful nor romantic. It is heaviness on the shoulders that breaks your spine in two. It is drowning in dark waters not knowing which way to swim up to for air. It is burning in the throat like the sting of a viper. It is poison slowly coursing through your blood as the despair numbs you into a meaningless abyss. It is the closest thing we have to a mental hell. Heartbreak is neither beautiful nor romantic.

I no longer wish you the best
I wish you what you deserve
For with this hope, I step back
And allow the universe to step in
And balance what should have been balanced long ago
The scales of justice that you tipped too low in your favor
Will one day be balanced
All that you did to me
And all that you gained from it will be measured
Gram by gram
And be given back
I wish you only what you deserve
It is no longer between you and me
It is now between you and yourself

                         -        the universe is watching

I pray
Oh God, I pray
She escapes way before I did

- run

The day that we die
Will be the day that
He who has hurt us most
Cries the loudest
He who did not want to say hello
Will come to say goodbye
Oh, what a day that day will be
But alas,
The punch line to this world's most cruelest joke is
That day we will not see

- too late

The more of them I meet
The more I am confused
Why they are the standard of strength

-     "be a man"

Maybe we have not listened to the devil's side of the story
Maybe there was a reason he wanted so desperately
To prove that men can be evil too

- two sides

Dear stomach, that has lost its grip
Every time I think of him
There will be a day I see
Where you will be calm and free
And on that day if I think of him
You will not hurt against my skin
You will not react ever again
To the painful memory of him
Instead I will think of spring
Of daffodils, friends, and ice cream
I will think of anything
And you'll leap with joy and sing
And maybe one day
There will be a guy
Who will give you butterflies
And that is the day you will be free
Of everything that you now cannot be

- queasy

How can I have come from the rib of man
If the rib of man is formed in my womb?

- woman

There is no responsibility greater than that of being a good person

- repeat after me

Dear reader,

I thank you for journeying with me amongst these clouds

Like each cloud in the sky, we hold within us sometimes storms and sometimes fresh air

I hope that you may find your way home

And that you enter it with a new light

And an understood soul

ABOUT THE AUTHOR

Melody Khosravi is an Iranian-American artist and psychology graduate. This is her debut on the written page.

Made in the USA
Lexington, KY
02 September 2019